Straits & Narrows

ALSO BY SIDNEY WADE

Stroke
From Istanbul
Celestial Bodies
Green
Empty Sleeves

Sidney Wade

Straits &

Narrows

poems

A Karen & Michael Braziller Book

PERSEA BOOKS / NEW YORK

Persea Books, Inc.
277 Broadway
New York, NY 10007

Library of Congress Cataloging-in-Publication Data
Wade, Sidney.
[Poems. Selections]
Straits & Narrows : Poems / Sidney Wade.
        pages cm.
Includes bibliographical references and index.
ISBN 978-0-89255-425-6 (original trade paperback : alk. paper)
I. Title. II. Title: Straits and Narrows.

PS3573.A337S74 2013
811'.54—dc23
                2012047054

First edition
Printed in the United States of America
Designed by Rita Lascaro

In loving memory of my parents,

Morris Leon Wade
(1919–1984)

Helen Rosalie Dahl Wade
(1920–1992)

Contents

Acknowledgments

Thanks to the editors of the following journals, in which the poems indicated previously appeared:

32 Poems: "Late"
cellpoems: "Corrective"
Lo-Ball: "Animist Manifesto"
National Poetry Review: "Coat Screws With Grease to Solve Woe,"
    "Geep"
Plume: "Amazed"
Poetry Congeries: "Interlude," "Such Luck"
The Birmingham Poetry Review: "Priairie," "Stuck"
The Cincinatti Review: "Peony"
The Hampden-Sydney Review: "In the Mood for Love,"
    "Dream Autobiography"
The Hopkins Review: "A dragonfly alights..."
The Rumpus: "Boulder," "all the new thinking..."

Gratitude and love to Poultry Group and to Lisa and my "boys," without whose help these poems and this manuscript would have contained a great many more infelicities: Joe Haldeman, Lola Haskins, Brandy Kershner; Geoff Brock, Michael Loughran, Randall Mann, and Lisa Zeidner. And to Gabe Fried, keen-eyed and wise. Thank you all.

Straits & Narrows

ANIMIST MANIFESTO

Where is God
we ask in haste

and answer slow
in winter-paced

adagio
in appetite

in thrum
and fissure

in pressure
in the deep-set

vein in silence and
in marbled sleep

in the garbled dream
of working men

with far-flung
shoulders in

the steady hum
of axled tires

in their endless
turning and

the slow burn
of their prose

in the autumn
poetry of fire

in the mordant
tones of blazery

in fall-stroked
polyphonic meadows

in the darkness
of the Dorian scale

the shadowed face
and tangled dance

that trails
all music

and its fragrance
in the winding

sonnetude
of grief

that punctures
every day's veneer

in all bodies bound
by gravity

in the splendor
of the soul-fish

floating in
their water holes

waiting patiently
for amplitude

for metaphor
for the song

of mind
made flesh

BOULDER

This world
is full

of beautiful
surprises

here's one
one bright

blue noon
on Loon

Lake I sat
on the porch

eating lunch
and watched

a chipmunk
on the compost

pile nibble
a strand

of spaghetti
until he'd

consumed
it all it

pleased
me well

to share
a meal

with such
congenial

company
and then

I heard
a tremendous

fluster
in the lake

a moose
had quietly

been munching
on underwater

plants fine
delicacies

to northern
ruminant types

and what
I had taken

to be a boulder
turned out

to have been
her shoulder

as her submerged
mouth hoovered

up all the juicy
stems of my water

lilies until
her hungry

lungs ached
for air

and she reared
her head

in a great
splendor

of bright water
a sloshing

slurping
slurry

of mud
and stems

profuse and
dripping

from her
streaming

maw as she
observed

me coolly
before

heading down
for more

INTERLUDE

The never-ending
meditation

continues
this early

morning
squirrels on

the porch
and in the trees

the lake is still
the silence

blue I've belled
the cat made

coffee and
am ready

with my pencil
to accept

whatever
mind imagines

is its music
or its body

or its gold
I've hung

the nyjer
thistle-seed

and am
waiting

for the cloud
of goldfinches

I hear is near
to appear

CORRECTIVE

Sorry
but
nature's
first
green
is
red
in
spite
of
what
Mr.
Frost
said

Gold
arrives
later
in
willow
and
birch
Red
like
blood
runs
last
and
first

SUCH LUCK

In the larger
darknesses

of the ground
west of sight

I'm shouting
at the mountain

of silence
and depth

when
an eye opens

and I open
my mouth

to devour
the sound

of night
which in time

will filter
through all

that swings
or hums

my fist
is full

of letters
my wrist

aches like
a drum

such luck
to hold

a compendium
of resonant

voices in
the sanatorium

of my head
whose guest-

book is
crowded

with the high-
brow and

the low-brow
and whose

overseer
in the back-

ground prays
every day

for my bright
daughters

and the black
blue waters

they're swimming
through and all

the possibilities
they might

swallow
and I know

my strength
and sphere

may be slight
but look

at this
handful

of light
I found

in a crack
in the ground

here
it's for you

IN THE MOOD FOR LOVE

Evening spills gold
onto the shoulders

of the trees
across the lake

the quiet air
wants me

out in it
but I remain

inside watching
a Chinese

movie *In
the Mood*

for Love
and now

my lover
calls from

the city and we
reimmerse

in the slow
dark warmth

of our recent
meeting and

now the lake
too is calling

to me I want
intensely

to soak
in that light

right now
and it occurs

to me a finite
amount

of golden
light

remains
to my life

as the red
squirrels

quarrel
on the porch

and I return
to the Chinese

movie which
concerns

adulterous
lovers

and naturally I
think of my own

adulterous
lover and see

again the fireflies
that lazily

surprised us
in the dusk

of the park
and the haze

of our bodies and
their accustomed

but ever more
profound pleasures

or should I say
understandings

and now some
children kayak

by in their
red and yellow

boats and their
calls and laughter

return me to
an evening

long ago on
this same lake

I'm rowing with
a handsome young

philosopher we're
one of a phalanx

of boats heading
to the western edge

of the lake in search
of a diabetic

boy lost
in the darkening

marsh and
the philosopher

and I are
ferrying

the game warden
whose body

odor powerful
as a corpse in heat

wafts back and chokes
us sniggling

at the oars
but he was the one

who found
the boy in

the impossibly
mosquitoed

northern swamp
and brought

him back and
now I'm back

to the movie
where a very

long moment
is devoted

to the smoke
that sensually

envelops
the handsome

lead and I
remember

the *Bodies*
exhibit we saw

in Tampa
the flayed

and disemboweled
corpses of many

Chinese dead
mounted

and posed
to instruct our

healthy western
children on

the intricate beauty
of the inner self

and we all
clearly saw

how most of these
exposed lungs

were charcoal
black and

now night has
truly fallen

the wind
has dropped and

the life-jacketed children
call to their life-jacketed

parents and
paddle on home

and in the Chinese
movie it sounds

like Nat King Cole
is crooning in

awkward
unaccustomed

Spanish to us all
as the sexy

smoke swirls
around the head

of the sexy
married man

and so much is lost
in translation

FORM

And now the lake's
slate-gray

the trees
green fringed

and deeper
in the distance

the mountain
hulks and presses

its blue form
insistent

on the eye
absolutely

everything
at stake

at every
moment

PRAIRIE

Everything
shines

the water
the grasses

sun and wind
and alligators

on the move
in the sink

moorhens
chuckle

and bleat
as the wings

of the boat-
tailed grackle

whoosh
and he purple

and royal blue
and green passes

through
this beautiful

high system
each creature

here pursues
another and

the beating
flailing thing

fights down
the gullet

to become
the shine on

another's wing
I wish

for equanimity
in the face

of this I want
to slide into

this great
grim maw

with the grace
of the gator

as he eases
himself onto

the bank
in the sun

and smiles
and creaks

just like
someone

settling into
a leather sofa

LATE

Our summer
was brilliant

and brief
we rejoiced

and shoveled
cheap gold

and trinkets
into our pockets

and millions
of landfills

grew like boils
now God

is singing
Turmoil

his favorite song
and throngs

are sleeping
in the frost

and dust
is falling in

the empty homes
of the homeless

who will curl
in the cold

with their children
and the breeze

all night long
will cover them

with a blanket
of fallen leaves

THE CREEPS

Today is just
like yesterday

except for
a swim

across
the lake

whose water
creeps

me out most
always has

since long ago
when I first

discerned
the rusty

devil's claws
in the shallows

under my
canoe

that seemed
to strain to leap

from the lake
bed up

to drag
me and my

tipsy craft
down in

their jagged
clutch

nevertheless
I jump

into the cold
black

water and tie
the swim

ring to my
ankle in case

of cramp
or worse what

could be worse
I'll tell you

it's when
you reach

the deep
interior

a quarter
mile

from either
solid shore

and that
dark beast

who's kept
to those

silent depths
forever

will look up
and notice

above him
in the blue

a feast
two naked legs

winking whitely
in the high

firmament
of his world

and who will
surely rise

to investigate
what might

be for him
a revelation

of flavor
and swirl

akin
to that

of an oyster
or maybe

a pearl
on toast

FAT AND LAZY

Lazy lazy lazy
in my fat

fat world
which on this

brilliant
day wrinkles

with a million
diamonds

prickling
the surface

of the lake
here's a breeze

riffling the face
of my mid-

morning snack
cream

of asparagus soup
and over here

the green cedars
are bobbing

in the wind see
their hundreds

of green hands
flutter and swoop

now it's no longer
enough to mutter

spiffy the children
have grown

and gone
and it's time

to tune
the throng

of words
beyond things

as they are
to meander

in the direction
of the grander

conjunction
the more

venerable
song

WILD RASPBERRY

On a muggy
summer day

in a very
buggy berry

patch
you find

a fine
plump

jewel
and reach

for it when
over there!

a huge
and dazzling

juicier morsel
bigger than

your thumb
hanging by

a spider's
thread

but as
you tug

on the now
humble nub

the sublimer
number falls

and is lost
forever

in that
murky

hole in
the dark

precarious
mess of

wet slash
and roots

beneath your
sorry feet

O

mountainous
appetite!

how flat
we'd find

the view
without you!

LITTORAL

A dragonfly
alights

beside me
on the dock

and cocks
his head

the better
to observe

the inert
and reddening

barge of flesh
looming large

above him
on this flawless

bright and windy
afternoon he's

not the flashy
type dull brown

with compound
ashy eyes

a bit rotunder
than the sky

blue dancer
with the black

and lacy wings
whose great

and fancy
beauty pings

the atmosphere
with instant

sapphire pleasure
when it deigns

to appear
and which

always brings
more than a whiff

of high art
to the party

I wonder
what he makes

of me this finely
bulging

little ounce
of God's intelligence

he might recall
Chagall's

Le Poète Alongé
and rightly suspect

I'd imbibed a wee
bit too much wine

last night
or maybe

he admires
my complicated

hues the
perforated

subtle
light-thrown

shadows
the staccato

under the radar
the tonal score

of a lucky
poet who

on good days
understands

the soul as form
of forms who also

lives in fear
of the possibility

that the gods
might have

no need
for her at all

or maybe he's
just resting

in the sun
his manifold

eyes transmitting
sixty million

times this vision
to his tiny

conscious mind:
light

on the horizon
that ever-porous

littoral where
the bright

bleeds through
the borders

of the darkening
shore

STAN'S TREES

In the green
haze of summer

in the blaze
of fall

in the great
white freeze

of winter
Stan saw

the forest
in the trees

his eye
and lens

took in
the bent

but unbroken
the grim

improbable roots
feeding

the frailest
of shoots

as his frame
shed its weight

his eye
grew large

and saw
straight

into the spirit
to live

he's gone
but he's left

us his prints
a shuffle

in red and
yellow leaves

an impress
in the moss

lavender shadows
in the snow

he has entered
the great woods

SOLITUDE

is silver
as yesterday's

weather
below

the low
winter ceiling

of clouds
the slant

November
sun skittered

across the lake
and into

the house
in two weeks

tiny flakes
will begin sifting

out of the gray
sky one by one

open the door
let the cats in

now as I pin
wet clothes

to the line
idiotically

happy in
the crisp

clear air
a Gray Jay

boldly
alights

five feet
from me

and politely
asks

to be fed
I tell him

to wait
right there

go into
the house

open the door
let the cats out

and return
with bread

which he eats
from my hand

as I fret
about lurking

cats quite certain
I shouldn't

encourage
this sort

of perilous
behavior

open the door
let the cats in

it isn't lonely
with cats

and birds
and a fire

in the fireplace
and on

a good day
laundry to hang

open the door
let the cats out

poems to write
poets to read

like Lew Welch
as he thanks

his woodpile
and thinks

he's turning
shack simple

like Han Shan
and Wittgenstein

and possibly
me

open the door
let the cats in

solitude flows
in narrow

pressured
straits as in

the bosphorus
whose green

currents
are layered

and profound
and run counter

to each other
so that if

a fisherman
casts his net

deep enough
the lower

current
will tow

his boat
upstream

open the door
let the cats out

a minute ago
I heard

a gunshot
and stepped

outside
to listen

all I hear now
is the slosh

of small waves
on the rocks

and water
dripping

onto pebbles
from the roof

open the door
let the cats in

In bright
slanted light

and on
windless days

in utter
silence

it becomes
clear

we all must
descend one

by one
into winter

open the door
let the cats out

HYBRID

All the new
thinking is

about energy
says my

new lover
as I wonder

about
the crowd

that hovers
in the green

inbetweenness
in my head

the energetic
crew who

speak unspoken to
who volunteer

non sequiturs
when I'm mining

for the deeper thing
the regal thing

they substitute
gumshoe hoedown

or *a fine toothcomb*
or if I ponder

a smart sonnet
on *The Institute*

of Forgetting
they'll offer

moth-eaten
feather-bedded

meat-balled
things then steer

me into Beer
Harbor and say

y'on y'one
and leave

me sprawled
unhouseled

in hybrid doubt
about the rough

and tumble of
this banquet hall

when all
I really itch

to do is
engrave

on a golden bowl
a soliloquy

on the physics
of the soul

that hilarious
white wave

on the tufted
dark of the sea

COAT SCREWS WITH
GREASE TO SOLVE WOE

It isn't tiddly
this non-ironic

little bubble—
it's a heart

burn formation
double

vision
in which

misprision
of verb

for noun
happily disturbs

the diplopia
It's fiddly

it's true
on the slope

slippery
of lubricious

soil
but it's also

deliciously
knurled

bejeweled
oiled

and slick
with hope

PEONY

Plump mother-lode
of pleasure

tight buds all
awash in ants

pink skirts ragged
at the edges

old-fashioned
bowl

of fragrance
palace of ants

and feathers
I watch

the rain come
and the shining

heads bow
under heavy

jewels
Petals fall

in clumps
and scatter

soft and slow
on the pock-

marked soil
I cup a blossom

in my hands
lower my head

and inhale the scent
of *mother mother mother*

SIDNEY IN FLORIDA TO
DOROTHY *IN MEDIAS RES*

Janet saw the wonder
on your face

minutes
after you'd passed

I hope you're
in medias res

waiting
in a garden say

on a beautiful shore
until you've made

your peace
once more

with leaving us
and this fine

and difficult place
to move

into the universe
as it truly must be

filled with souls
who never really left

Bud Buno
Jenny parents

and cousins
and old old friends

everyone in fact
who has ever lived

from near and far
and long ago

free of your crooked
old frame

now you can dive
and swim

as sleek as an otter
your beautiful

green eyes wide
in that dazzling water

in that unimaginable
depth and beauty

seeing it true
we miss you

STUCK

The great blue
heron balances

on water
weeds

and pulls
at a long

dead stick
I've seen

him fly
these bones

into the high
dead tree

to build
his rigid nest

but this one
is truly stuck

no

he's pulling
at the body

of a cornsnake
whose tail

is knotted
firmly around

the stick his
head and half

his body
already

far down
the gullet

the heron can't
unknot the tail

so he
regurgitates

the top half
to work

a better angle
and now

the snake
dangles

limply as
the great bird

gnaws the gold-
red knot

with his hard
yellow beak

and swallows
again

an hour passes
the bird works

the cornsnake
clings the sun

shines
the wind

blows kites
and egrets

hawks and
swallows

soar in
the brilliant

light
of this

design
in which

every
bird

and every
beast

is obliged
to feast

on the living
to live

AMAZED

Today on
the windy

prairie
black clouds

sheet down
in the east

I'm going
to get wet

the blue-eyed
grass clumps

in tuffets
beside

the path
they startle

the corner
of the eye

like the swish
of an unseen

snake through
dry weeds

quick-turns
the head

a large
turtle naps

on the mud
bank

in the placid
shadow

of a torpid
alligator

it rains
a little

and I get
a little

wet with
the black-

necked stilts
who yap

like dogs
in swift

flight
over this

wet-bright
landscape

where
a single

whooping
crane slogs

in the shallow
marsh

hunting
for brunch

and thrusts
its fine red-

knotted
head into

the muck
and emerges

in black-face
and blinks

and we are
all amazed

RUN ON

Caveat emptor:

we'll be running
on together

for a while
and I'll

be carving up
the spiritual

possibilities in
the background

and we might
find from time

to time a reprise
of that old sublime

and unhappy opera
The Roaring

Desire for More
which is after all

the dire
wilderness

we all tend
to navigate

with tender
regard for

our poor
poor hands

so here's the plan
I'll serve as

the bravura conduit
to intuitionland

and you provide
the filthy lucre

and we'll orchestrate
a balanced dance

accompanied perhaps
by some nuanced

romantic fumbling
and maybe even

some Christian
death-threats

from the right
side of the brain

which is the nurse
douloureux

of macaronic
verse

o caro babbino now
don't you feel

better not really
that nurse is standing

on her histrionic
feet and yelling that

a wolfowitz in shit's
clothing is marauding

in our fold a vast
and uncurtailed

misprision of vision
o la! le pauvre

he and his pals
ace the tests

of violence and shame
every time they take

them then they
stash the crude

oil under the bed
what a tired old

cliche they
should be taking

care of the waifs
and the orphans

instead they
congregate

at the mouth
of the bible factory

outlet I *ask* you
what is this great

and golden whirl
a-coming to? or

what is the chief
effect of this pageant

as Mr. Stevens very late
of Hartford asks

as did my great
friend Hugh

more newly late
of Hartford gone

on New Year's Eve
he strapped on

skis and glided
over the thinnest

merest whisper
of new ice

which failed him
then immobilizing

cold gathered
him slow

in its heavy
arms and now

on this the brighter
side of the divide

we're poorer by
one vivid loving

slight and wiry
barefoot man

bandannaed
wild-haired fond

of smoke and poems
and I wonder how

the lanyard
of history

will tether this
single glazing loss

to the catalogue
of misery

it so surely
is compiling

in its always
forthcoming

great long
poem

MY ISTANBUL

My great blue
metropolis

of shadow and
of molten

dream my city
whose fabric

is constructed
of curious timbres

manhole covers
and nimble

historical seams
my city where grit

and beauty flash
in the windows

in transcendent
flares that

february forth
their slow revelations

as great green
accelerating mystery

muscles up
from the depths

of the hurrying
Bosphorus currents

my schizophrenic
city passionate

in it melancholy
and its keen

acquisitive ache
it glowers brightly

in its layers
of wool and gray

stone and linens
a splendid symphony

in minor key
home to riven

souls and ragged
beggars home

to the many
instruments

of poetry home
to polyspeak

whose pyrotechnic
frigidities dazzle

the spirit it's
out of control

it's out of this
world and

absolutely
fine

GEEP

The music
of the sleepy

day was
ravagingly

dull until
Michael reeled

up a *geep*
from the depths

of his considerable
intelligence

a *geep!*
a wonky blend

of goat and sheep
a medical medley

genetic fugue
they call *chimera*

another wholly
enthralling sound

we found
when googling *geep*

whose enharmonic
bleating in the end

rings oh so
sad the photo

on the screen
reveals a downcast

baby creature
neither here

nor there
two bold

and mordant
sets of chromosomes

whistling fortissimo
through its patch-work

hide a botched-up
map of silken hair

and wooly yellow
fur its forlorn

droopy ears
a study

in radical
embarrassment

I feel profoundly
sorry for this

border folly
this lonely little

instrument
of the ever-

expanding notion
of what's possible

but then I see
we're kin

the little *geep* and me
we're marginal

ephemera
intoning low

invisible messages
at the edges

of the known
to who knows

whom
the difference

between us
a matter of degree

the poet of course
a hybrid creature

of transport and remorse
an over-reacher

in semaphore
who knows that sound's

the gold in the ore
whose pleasure-ground

is linguistic welter
who rides like ice

on its own melting
to paradise

or to a stranger land
we don't yet understand

About the Author

SIDNEY WADE (www.sidneywade.com) is the author of five previous poetry collections, most recently Stroke. Her poems and translations appear in *The New Yorker, The Paris Review, Poetry,* and elsewhere. She lives in Gainesville, where she is Professor of English at the University of Florida, and in the Rangeley Lakes region of Maine.